MAKE MONEY NOW!™

MONEY-MAKING OPPORTUNITIES FOR TEENS WHO ARE ARTISTIC

GINA HAGLER

ROSEN PUBLISHING®
New York

To Judith

Published in 2014 by The Rosen Publishing Group, Inc.
29 East 21st Street, New York, NY 10010

First Edition

Library of Congress Cataloging-in-Publication Data

Hagler, Gina.
Money-making opportunities for teens who are artistic/Gina Hagler.—
First Edition.
pages cm.—(Make money now!)
Includes bibliographical references and index.
ISBN 978-1-4488-9387-4 (library binding)
1. Vocational guidance—Juvenile literature. 2. Money-making projects for children—Juvenile literature. 3. Art—Vocational guidance—Juvenile literature. 4. Teenagers—Employment—Juvenile literature. 5. Job hunting—Juvenile literature. I. Title.
HF5381.2.H34 2013
331.702—dc23

2012045606

Manufactured in the United States of America

CPSIA Compliance Information: Batch #S13YA: For further information, contact Rosen Publishing, New York, New York, at 1-800-237-9932.

CONTENTS

INTRODUCTION

When ten-year-old Maddie Bradshaw wanted to decorate her middle school locker with magnets, she had a problem. She couldn't find any magnets she liked. To solve the problem, she took some bottle caps from her uncle's old-fashioned soda machine, created her own designs, and attached the bottle caps to magnets to create custom magnets. Her friends loved them so much that she gave some to them.

It wasn't long before Maddie wanted to enjoy her bottle cap designs outside of school. She created a necklace that made it easy to swap the bottle caps whenever she liked. Her friends also loved the necklaces—so much so that Maddie decided to take fifty of the necklaces and bottle caps to a local toy store to see if it would sell them. The store agreed to carry them on consignment. (The store's owners didn't buy them from her outright, but they agreed to display them, and they would keep a percentage of the sale price as a commission if they sold.) When all fifty necklaces and bottle caps sold out within two hours, Maddie knew it wasn't just her friends who loved her creations.

With the help of her mother, Maddie created a company called m3 Girl Designs. For her initial supplies, Maddie invested $300 of her own money, and her mother pitched in $300 to match that amount. Today, their initial investment of $600 has grown into a company with several million dollars in yearly revenue. Employees in Texas make all the company's products by hand. Maddie and her younger sister, Margot, still create each bottle cap design.

Friendship bracelets are one of many types of jewelry you can create and sell.

Maddie serves as the president and head designer and Margot as the vice president and assistant designer. The company is named for Maddie, Margot, and Mom. It's a limited liability company (LLC), and Maddie and Margot share the profits equally. The next big step for m3 Girl Designs is licensing. Maddie is currently exploring licensing opportunities that will put her designs on items other than bottle caps. She still loves to draw. In an interview with Nate Berkus on his television show, she offered the following advice: "Just make sure whatever you do is your passion."

Jewelry making is just one option available to artistic teens who want to start a business. There are many other ways to put artistic talent to profitable use. In the following sections, we'll talk about ways to make your own opportunities through entrepreneurship. We'll look at the ins and outs of running your own business and identify some of the resources that are available to help you turn your creative ideas into success. We'll also explore traditional jobs connected to your interests and show you how to use internship and volunteer opportunities as a first step to the career of your dreams. At the end, there is a list of resources that may be helpful as you try to put your artistic talents to work.

CHAPTER 1

Be an Entrepreneur

Pet sitting is just not your thing. Neither is car washing, homework helping, or lawn mowing. You're either too young for a job, or the ones you can get, such as bagging groceries or serving fast food, are not appealing. Still, you need to make some money.

Fortunately, you're artistic. You can draw and paint. You can sculpt and create mosaics. You can make jewelry and other accessories. In fact, there are many things you can think of to create with your hands and some art supplies. Plus, doing projects that use your artistic talents is a lot of fun. Someday, you plan to work in an art-related field, such as graphic design or computer animation. So what's keeping you from putting your artistic talents to work right now? Believe it or not, you can get paid for doing what you love while you are still a teenager.

FIND YOUR NICHE

The first step is finding your niche—the place in the market that only you can occupy. Maybe your original anime characters are huge favorites with your friends. Maybe everyone who sees the mural you've drawn on your bedroom wall falls in love with it. Maybe your latest jewelry draws admirers every time. Whatever it is that sets you apart from the crowd is just the thing to make your own opportunity.

There is a trick to finding a good niche. It needs to be specific enough that people can appreciate the uniqueness of

If painting is your passion, find a way to turn your artwork into a business.

what you do, yet broad enough that a lot of people will consider your services. While you are trying to find your niche, take some time to think about the things you love to create. Then think about the reactions your friends and others have to your creations. Chances are good that if they are excited about your work, paying customers will be, too. Get some of your friends to brainstorm with you. No idea is too crazy. Encourage people to tell you what they like most or what they would like to see you create. At the end of the brainstorming session, you'll have a list of ideas to explore.

Suppose everyone agrees that your murals are terrific. A quick search shows that lots of artists do murals. What sets you apart from those other artists? Do you want to be known as the person who does murals in nurseries? How about the person who does murals in children's bedrooms? Maybe you can see yourself creating murals in playrooms in people's homes or in public play spaces.

Let's say you are drawn to the idea of creating art for a room where kids go to have fun. Maybe you'll decide your niche is making fanciful wall murals for playrooms. Spend some time doodling and see what you come up with. If you like creating animals and figures, include some that the children in a particular house might enjoy. For instance, do the children you know love dragons? Jungle animals? Create some samples. Use bright colors and images in your mural to make the playroom an inviting space.

On the other hand, maybe you are crazy about anime. You love to create characters and make up stories about them. Perhaps your niche is making graphic novels that feature your characters. You could create handmade books to sell on the comics market. Or, you might create large, inked drawings of your anime characters in action, suitable for framing and hanging. It's up to you to define your niche. Once you do, you will be known as the person who creates that type of art.

To generate business as a muralist, do a project in a visible location, such as a child care center, school, or camp.

GET YOURSELF OUT THERE

Once you've decided upon your niche, it's time to do some networking and see if your idea might meet the needs of paying customers.

First, you'll need to gather polished samples of your work that you can show potential clients. For example, if your niche is doing playroom murals, consider offering free services as a muralist in exchange for a photograph of the completed mural and references from the client. Make sketches of other murals you could create for clients. Include some drawings you think boys would like, some that girls would like, some that are not gender-specific, and some that are for very young children. If you are open to a variety of styles, include several styles in your samples. Put all your samples in a binder or portfolio case. Make sure this collection is easy for potential clients to browse.

Perhaps graphic art is your niche, and you are interested in designing logos for small businesses. There are many sources for small business owners to order customized business cards, stationery, and other materials using premade formats and graphics. However, most would prefer to have something that is unique. Gather some samples of your work, perhaps designs you created for friends or relatives, and then approach some small businesses with them. If you're not sure how to find small business owners, see if your local chamber of commerce or small business center can help you.

IS YOUR IDEA A BUSINESS?

Not every idea is a business. And not every business idea is successful. For an idea to succeed as a business, it has to provide a solution to a problem shared by a lot of people. Further, the entrepreneur has to be able to solve that problem for people at a reasonable cost and still make a profit.

For instance, your idea might be to create one-of-a-kind murals for nurseries for triplets. Is that a viable business? How many triplets are born each month in your town? The answer is likely not very many. On the other hand, painting custom murals for all nurseries can meet any parents' need to create a welcoming space for a new baby. This idea has a lot more business potential.

Let's say you decide to create your murals with materials that are baby-safe but among the most expensive materials available. Is that going to appeal to potential customers? Could you create a mural with materials that are just as baby-safe but less expensive? The goal is to create a stunning mural, not to create a mural that is so expensive that no one will pay the price.

By defining your niche, identifying your potential customers, and considering the cost of the solution, you will see quickly if your idea is a business. Remember, the goal is to use your artistic talent to create something of value to a steady stream of potential customers. Without the customers, you might have a terrific idea, but you won't have a business.

GO ONLINE

Instead of providing art-related services, maybe you can create unique craft items to sell on the Internet. You may be talented at making decorated clothing, personalized baby gifts, or custom models, just to name a few. Some artistic teens start their own online stores or participate in existing online stores, such as Etsy.com, to sell this type of merchandise.

Entrepreneur Jessica Plymate sews creative designs onto vintage and recycled clothes. She sells them on Etsy.com and other sites.

Embellished, or decorated, clothing can include a vast array of items from painted or ribbon-adorned T-shirts to stenciled sneakers and bejeweled jeans. If you're not sure what will sell, you can create samples to put on a site. You'll quickly see what sells and what doesn't.

If you are good at making custom models, check out what's selling at the local hobby shop. While some people like creating models themselves, someone who is creating an entire fleet or army might welcome the chance to have some of the work done for him.

Baby items are always in demand. Painted step stools have been popular for generations. So have blocks or other items that spell out the baby's name. (You must be sure to use paints that are nontoxic and baby-safe.)

Whatever product you choose, make sure there is something about it that makes it unique.

Creating an online store may sound complicated, but it doesn't have to be. You can set up your store using a free blogging application. Your products can be displayed as images and descriptions within blog posts. You can categorize your posts and then use the categories as the menu items on the blog. Customers can then click on T-shirts, for example, and see all the different designs you have for sale. To place an order, customers can contact you through a form on the site or at an e-mail address you create for your business. To accept payment, you can establish a merchant account with PayPal.

ART + KIDS = OPPORTUNITY

Some artistic teens who enjoy working with kids decide to combine their artistic talents with child-care services to create their niche. For example, they may provide an art activity with each babysitting assignment. Some of the projects may take more than one babysitting visit to complete. Others can be completed in one night or afternoon. These teens can charge more than a typical babysitter because they offer additional value. Also, they're likely to be in higher demand. Parents are happy because their kids are doing something creative. Kids are happy because they have something fun to do. It's a win-win all around. To give parents an idea of what types of projects you can do with their children, make several project boxes. In

Doing an art project with the children you babysit gives the children an enjoyable activity. It also enhances your value as a babysitter.

each box, include the materials that you will use in the activity and a finished sample.

Summer activities, school-break camps, and group babysitting on weekends are additional services you can offer parents. Offer your services for several hours as an art camp or workshop. The children can choose from a variety of projects. If the camp is ongoing, pick a different theme each week. Have the campers create a variety of items based on that theme. At the end of the week, invite the parents to an art show with the completed work on display. Once again, samples of the types of projects you offer will be an important part of your marketing efforts. If some of the projects are large or complicated, include a photo of a finished project or a description of what the project will entail.

Birthday parties are another great opportunity for artistic and entrepreneurial teens. You can lead the guests in doing a craft project at the party. Or, you can offer

Participating in a craft activity is a lot of fun for birthday party guests.

your services to create custom party favors and decorations. Customers can have the best of both worlds if you lead the children in creating their own party favors. The party will be special because of the art activity you provide. The favors will be special because the kids created them. As part of your marketing, present samples of the favors guests can create. People will want to see examples of your ideas before they decide to hire you for their child's party.

Once you decide upon a niche that will support a business, you are on your way to becoming an entrepreneur. Remember that opportunities are all around you. The important thing is the ability to recognize and seize these opportunities.

CHAPTER 2

TRADITIONAL JOBS FOR ARTISTIC TEENS

Not everyone is ready to jump right in and start a business. For many teens, getting a traditional job—one in which you are employed as an artist by an existing business—is more appealing. If you're the kind of person who prefers a traditional job with steady hours and pay, your chances of finding a position depend on your age, the type of work, and the competition for the job.

LOOKING FOR A JOB

A positive attitude is the most important thing you'll need when looking for a job that uses your artistic abilities. You are going to meet a lot of people in your search for a job. Some of the people will be in a position to help you. Others will not. All of them will form an impression of you. Since you'll be looking for jobs that use your talents many times over the years, it makes sense to make a good impression. Here are some tips for successful networking and job searching:

- Dress appropriately when looking for a job. This is not the time for cutoff jeans and a ratty T-shirt. Wear something you feel comfortable in, but make sure it is nicer than what you wear to attend school or to go out with your friends.
- Bring a business card with you. The card should have your name, e-mail address, and phone number. You can

buy perforated, blank business cards and create and print your own. You can also use an online service to create and print your own design. Whatever you decide, create a card in a font that's easy to read.

- Make eye contact with the person you're speaking to. Speak clearly. Offer your hand for a handshake when you first meet. Introduce yourself. Explain that you're looking for a job that will use your artistic talents. Turn your phone off and leave it in your pocket.
- Think ahead about what you'll say about yourself and your experience. It's helpful to prepare a short pitch that describes the top skills you have to offer. Practice it in front of the mirror.
- Bring along samples of your work in a notebook or portfolio.
- Bring a pen in case you need to complete an application. Ask your neighbors or teachers ahead of time if you can use them as references. If they say yes, ask them for a telephone number you can include on the application.

Showing enthusiasm and leaving a positive first impression are important parts of getting a job.

Even if someone does not have a job for you right now, leaving your contacts with a positive impression of you is important. Then when they do have an appropriate opportunity—or learn of an opening that someone else wants to fill—you will be high on the list of candidates.

WHERE TO APPLY

Think about the kinds of organizations that might need a person with artistic abilities. You'll be surprised at how many businesses and nonprofits can use your skills. The opportunities range from the after-school program at a local elementary school to the weekly programs held at your local arts or community center. Many religious schools also include art in their weekly education programs. Ask your friends and relatives about the programs they participate in, or the programs they participated in when they were younger, as a way of learning about local programs that include art. You can also browse directories of community resources online, such as on your local Patch site.

AFTER-SCHOOL PROGRAMS

After-school programs are good places for artistic teens to look for jobs. Some of these programs focus specifically on art. Instructors can often use an assistant to prepare and distribute supplies or to work with small groups of children within the larger group.

To find out where art programs are held after school, check the Web site of your local school or school district. The PTA (Parent-Teacher Association) portion of the Web site may be especially helpful. It may offer flyers or details for the programs. If there are no art after-school programs available, maybe there is a general after-school program that could use your talents. Such programs usually include art in their activities.

Call the program's director or organizer and ask if you can stop by and introduce yourself. Think about what you want to say beforehand. Practice a few times before you make the call. Make some notes that you can refer to as you speak. Then relax and pretend you're speaking to the parent of a friend. If the director agrees to meet with you, be prepared. For an art program, bring a sample of your work. For a general after-school program, bring a sample and some ideas for the projects you would do with the children.

CHILD LABOR LAWS

Federal child labor laws, starting with the Fair Labor Standards Act (FLSA) of 1938, were enacted to protect children from unsafe working conditions and long hours that left no time for education or proper rest.

Federal law has different regulations for fourteen- and fifteen-year-olds than it does for sixteen- and seventeen-year-olds. Basically, the hours that a younger teen can work are fewer than the hours for an older teen. Also, the types of work a fourteen- or fifteen-year-old can do are subject to greater restrictions than the types of work a sixteen- or seventeen-year-old can do.

The good news for artistic teens is that federal labor regulations list "work of an intellectual or artistically creative nature" as work that is not prohibited for fourteen- and fifteen-year-olds. You'll still need to check the provisions of your state's child labor laws. Specifically check the description of work of an artistically creative nature and the age at which teens are eligible for that work. Also check to see the number of hours and times of day that you can work, the rates you can be paid, and whether or not you'll need any working papers or permits—and how to get them. If you're still not sure about the rules, check with your school's guidance counselor. The guidance department may have the information you need.

ARTS CENTERS

You can also consider applying for a job at a nonprofit arts center. Local and regional arts centers usually provide a number of arts opportunities in the form of classes or camps. Some of these programs are for children and others are for adults. On weekends and holidays, there may also be parent-child classes. Any of these classes might need an assistant.

Check the center's schedule and see which programs fit with your talents. For example, many arts centers have a darkroom that could use teens with experience in photography. They are sure to have drawing and painting classes. Pottery classes, in which students throw their own pots before glazing them, are another common offering at an arts center. Sculpture is often offered, too. Prepare some samples of your work and arrange a time to stop by to introduce yourself.

A community darkroom may be able to use your experience.

COMMUNITY AND RECREATION CENTERS

Even if your town or city doesn't have an arts center, it may have a community or recreation center. Community centers are usually funded and run by the city, by a nonprofit agency, or by a religious organization. In addition to programs for youth, many of these centers offer programs for the elderly. There may even be a senior center in your community. If you like spending time communicating with and helping older people, this may be a great option for you. Check out your local community or senior center and see what programs are offered. Then think of some projects that might work for this age group before putting together samples of your work and stopping by.

Recreation centers and city or countywide recreation programs are likely to offer art and craft classes for a variety of ages. Again, check what is being offered, match it with your abilities and interests, and apply for a job. With your talent and enthusiasm for art, you will be an excellent addition.

RELIGIOUS SCHOOLS

Religious schools are schools run by churches, synagogues, and other houses of worship to provide education about religion. Many religious schools have classes after school or on weekends that include art projects. Those near you might need some help. Check the Web site for the religious institution. Try to locate the name of the principal of the school, as well as the name of the art teacher, if the school has one. These individuals may have phone numbers or e-mail addresses listed. Try to arrange a time to stop by and meet one or both of these people. As with your other applications, be sure to provide samples of your work and some information about why you would be an excellent person for the job.

PRESENTING YOURSELF

The way you present yourself makes a difference in whether or not you are offered a job. A positive attitude and appropriate dress are helpful in making a good first impression. It's also important to showcase your qualifications for the job. Your portfolio, résumé, and work samples are essential to this effort. Bringing these materials demonstrates that you are serious about the opportunity. Remember that anything you bring must be in a form that reflects well on you. Take the time to proofread your materials and display them in a neat and organized fashion.

PORTFOLIO

As an artist, your portfolio is your calling card. It is an introduction to who you are as an artist. Because of this, it's essential that the work you choose for your portfolio is work you are proud of. To increase your chances of landing a job, it's a good idea to include work in more than one genre. For instance, if you are a photographer, bring along prints that illustrate the kind of work you do. It might be black-and-white work that you developed yourself or digital work that you edited with photo-editing software. If you also sketch or paint, bring along work that represents your abilities in that genre. If you make mosaics, pottery, stained glass, or sculpture, you can include some of those pieces in your portfolio as well. It doesn't make sense to lug around larger creations, but including images that show the intricacies of your work will be just right.

If you can afford one, purchase a portfolio case at an art supply store. There are many different types. Pick the one that is the best size for your work. If a portfolio case is too expensive, buy some page protector sleeves and put your work in a binder. Be sure that your work is organized and neat.

Include work in your portfolio that gives potential employers a sense of who you are and what you do.

RÉSUMÉ

As a teen, you probably don't have a lot of professional experience to include in a résumé. But you do have classes you've taken, camps or special programs you've attended, and projects you've worked on. Put your name and contact information at the top of a typed page that includes this information. Break the information into categories, such as classes, summer programs, and projects. List the name and date of each program. Include a brief summary of the program or project in a line or two—just enough to give someone skimming the résumé a good idea of what you did. Explain what you accomplished during the course of the program. If you've received any awards or other forms of recognition, include them in a separate section at the bottom. Also include any special art programs you have participated in at school or outside school. The idea is to give the person reading your résumé a good idea of what you've accomplished in the art field.

INTERVIEW SKILLS

You already know that making a good first impression is important. Making eye contact, offering to shake hands, introducing yourself, and speaking clearly—these are the minimum you'll need to do to get a job. To really win over the interviewer, you'll need to answer questions in a way that clearly connects your personal qualities, experiences, and artistic talents to the particular job being offered. You want to show the interviewer that you can meet the demands of the position and solve problems for him or her.

If you're asked why you are the ideal candidate, be sure to mention that you're a hard worker, you learn quickly, you're eager for this opportunity, and you're excited to put your talents to work. Sincere enthusiasm and energy count for a lot. If you're asked about a past mistake, you can tell the interviewer what it was. Just be sure to include what you learned from the experience.

If your work has intricate details, be sure to include close-up photos in your portfolio.

WORK SAMPLES

If you are suggesting new projects or programs for an organization, it may be helpful to bring along a sample of the finished product you are suggesting. Maybe it will be a treasure box or a decorated journal. You might bring a treasure box, a decorated journal, or a string bracelet or anklet. Whatever it is, pick something that will communicate your talents and your understanding of the goals of the program. If the project is large, a series of images may be more practical than a sample. Use your judgment. Remember, you're there to introduce yourself, make a positive impression, present some of your work, and explain why you're the perfect person to hire. Everything you tell and show the interviewer should help to make this case.

CHAPTER 3

Internships and Volunteer Positions

Perhaps being an entrepreneur isn't for you. And in a tight job market, perhaps you've struck out in your search for a paying job. Why not consider a position as an intern or volunteer? You may not be paid for your time, but this kind of opportunity can help you gain the experience you need for the future. You can use your talents to do work you enjoy while taking steps toward the career you hope to have one day. You'll also have some interesting experiences to discuss in your college applications and essays. The more committed you are to your volunteer work or internship, the more you'll gain from it. Your growth will be evident when you talk about it, too.

INTERNSHIPS

An internship is an opportunity to work for a business or organization before you are old enough or have all the qualifications needed to be hired there. An internship may or may not be a paid position. People seek internships as a way of gaining experience in the field they hope to enter one day. Many different organizations offer internships that are of interest to teens with artistic talent.

Museums often have internship programs for those interested in careers as curators, museum educators, or other museum professionals. Artistic interns may also work on the exhibits in museums, aquariums, zoos, nature centers, and

An internship is a great way to learn about museum work. Before an interview, research the museum and its programs. Then relax and communicate why you are the ideal candidate.

other public places. They also may work on set design and props for live theater.

The community organizations near you may offer internships for artistic teens. One way to find out is to visit your school's guidance office and ask about internship opportunities. Another way is to ask your art teachers. You can also research organizations on your own. Check the Web sites of institutions where you'd like to work and see if they have any information about internships. Or call the organizations and ask to speak to a human resources hiring professional. That person should be able to tell you about the organization's internship opportunities or direct you to someone else who can. If all of that fails, try calling the department that does the type of work you are interested in, and see if you can arrange an internship that way.

VOLUNTEERING

Volunteering is a great way to gain experience. It is also a terrific way to learn to work with people. You'll have a supervisor, fellow volunteers, and people that you lead in art projects or do artistic work for. There are a lot of different possibilities, and each of them is an opportunity for you to develop valuable skills.

Serving as a volunteer is also a great way to become involved in your community. You'll meet people you might never have known—dedicated people who are making a difference in your area. You'll work on worthy projects while using your talents.

How do you find volunteer opportunities that are right for you? Checking with your guidance counselor is a great first step. Approaching organizations that do the type of work you're interested in is another way. The important thing is to keep your eyes open. Think about how you'd like to use your artistic talents. Then think about organizations or other places where this type of work is done. When you have a match, ask if there are volunteer opportunities. Chances are very good that a volunteer with your talents will be welcome.

OPPORTUNITIES THROUGH SCHOOL

Many schools have mandatory volunteer requirements for their students. If your school has this requirement, it is likely to have a list of organizations that are preapproved for student volunteers. Check to see whether any of these organizations are looking for teens with artistic ability. You may find there's a perfect fit between what you love to do and what an organization needs.

If you have skills in graphic art, you can gain practical experience by volunteering at a nonprofit organization.

In addition, many schools offer student service learning (SSL) as an option for students or as a requirement for graduation. Student service learning is an education method that links academic learning with student service that benefits the community.

Both volunteering and service learning can provide opportunities for artistic teens to get valuable real-world experience. For example, many nonprofits have volunteer positions that use artistic ability. You might design flyers for an upcoming event, help with a brochure that will be mailed to potential donors, or create art activities for children. Any of these projects can provide you with finished products for your portfolio. At the same time, you'll have the chance to help a nonprofit that wouldn't otherwise have access to someone with your talent.

COMMUNITY VOLUNTEER ORGANIZATIONS AND YOUTH GROUPS

Your community may have volunteer organizations that bring meals to the homebound elderly or provide babysitting for working mothers. It's likely one of these organizations could use the services of a teen with artistic ability. You might design posters that publicize the group's work or greeting cards the organization could use to raise funds. You might create coloring pages to entertain children. Taking the time to learn about volunteer organizations in your community is a great way to discover a place for you and your talents.

Youth groups, such as 4-H and scouting, offer programs and merit badges in the arts. For instance, 4-H offers an entire curriculum for those who are interested in the visual art of photography. Boy Scouts of America offers merit badges in basketry, drafting, graphic arts, landscape architecture, leath-

SCHOOL CLUBS AND EXTRACURRICULAR ACTIVITIES

When looking for ways to apply your skills, don't forget to explore the clubs and extracurricular activities available at your school. If there isn't an art club, see if you can start one. If you're interested in painting on a large scale, volunteer to work on the sets of the next high school theater production. Don't look at art as something that will be a big part of your life "someday." Find a way to make what you love a part of your daily life right now.

erwork, model design and building, painting, photography, pottery, sculpture, welding, and woodworking. Similarly, there are plenty of art opportunities for girls through the Girl Scouts of the USA. For instance, there are merit badges in woodworking, book art, digital movie making, and comic art. Any of these programs provide an opportunity for you to learn more about an area of art that interests you.

VOLUNTEERING TO HONE SKILLS

Another way to approach volunteer opportunities is to think of the skills you'd like to have for the future. Which skills are important for your college application? Which skills are essential to your future job prospects? Once you've identified these skills, you'll be in a better position to find a volunteer position or internship that will give you the chance to develop them.

For example, you might dream of working in video game design in the future. With your artistic skills, you can create amazing characters in an elaborate setting. The local community

Your talents may be just what the local ceramics studio is seeking.

college may offer a class in video game design that focuses on programming. Perhaps you could offer your artistic skills to the class. In exchange for designs that bring the visual part of the game to life, you could participate in the class and learn about the programming involved. Opportunities like this are worth exploring.

If ceramics is your thing, you could volunteer to help customers with more ambitious projects at the local ceramics store. Many towns have stores where people make and glaze their own pottery or decorate ready-made items. But many of the people who participate don't have a lot of art experience. There are a number of different ways to create special effects, but many customers don't know how to execute them. Your volunteer efforts would give you experience with these effects. It would also give you experience teaching and working with others.

PARLAYING EXPERIENCE INTO SUCCESS

By the end of a summer or semester of volunteering or interning, you will have some serious experience, as well as evidence to help document your accomplishments. In addition, you will have many transferable skills that you can use in volunteer or paid positions in the future.

AN EXPANDED PORTFOLIO

Your portfolio will definitely grow as a result of your volunteer work. You'll have pictures of your projects to include in your portfolio. If you worked with groups of adults or kids, include photos of yourself interacting with them if you can. It will give someone leafing through your portfolio the chance to fully understand your role and what you contributed as a volunteer.

If some of your artwork is elaborate or detailed, take photos that show those artistic touches. You can include close-up shots along with photos that show the work in its entirety. If your role was to teach others, you can show examples of your students' art to demonstrate the results of your instruction.

Remember, your portfolio tells the story of your work. Be sure your artistic talent and creativity speak.

EXPERIENCE WORKING WITH PEOPLE

Employers and colleges want candidates who are self-motivated and able to work well independently. However, these qualities alone are not everything you'll need. The ability to work well with others has been important since your very first playgroup or preschool experience. You'll also need to show future employers and colleges that you work well with others.

Volunteer projects, like the painting of this mural in Los Angeles, give you the opportunity to work as part of a team.

As an adult professional, you'll often work on large projects that include a number of people. The people may be from one group or department, or from several. If you have a reputation for being a good communicator or team player with a lot of talent, you will be an artist in demand.

Your volunteer and internship experiences provide you with several types of people skills. The first is your ability to work with and for your supervisor. The second is your ability to cooperate with other staff or volunteers to get a job done. Another is your ability to relate to the individuals or groups you are serving. Having proven experience in these areas to include in your college application, résumé, or skills summary is important.

REFERENCES

In addition to learning new skills, working with others, and using your talents to help a worthy cause, volunteering or interning can also be a source of references. References are people who can attest to your strengths in letters of recommendation or in phone conversations with future employers.

It may be a while before you need a letter of recommendation that is geared toward a specific job or opportunity. However, it's a good idea to ask for a general letter of recommendation at the end of your time as a volunteer or intern, while your work is still fresh in your supervisor's mind. He or she can describe your responsibilities and a bit about the way you carried them out. Include the letter in your portfolio.

Your references may also be in a position to tell you about other opportunities, now and in the future. Make sure you ask for some time to speak with your supervisors about what you hope to do with your artistic talents in the future. Thank them for the opportunity to work with and learn from them, and check in with them occasionally after you leave. If they are working in positions that use their own artistic talents, they'll certainly understand what it takes to get started. If you are talented and eager, and have done good work for them, it's likely they'll be happy to help you as you try to launch your career.

CHAPTER 4

STARTING AND RUNNING AN ART-RELATED BUSINESS

You've decided to start your own business to create ceramic pieces with custom designs. Some of the pieces will be mugs with creative images and sayings. Some will be personalized plates that are designed as birthday or wedding presents. You'll also be selling baby sets that include a bowl, plate, and cup. Canisters and special-purpose bowls and platters are also on your list of products.

You feel confident that you can produce ceramic pieces that are going to sell. There's just one thing: knowing how to create a fantastic product and knowing how to run a business are two different skill sets. If you are going to be doing this on your own, you need to learn some business basics that will enable you to keep good records and make a profit.

YOUR BUSINESS PLAN

A business plan is a good way to think through your idea from start to finish. You can use special software that helps you prepare a basic business plan. If you are starting a small, simple business, you can first prepare a plan that covers the most important aspects of a successful business. As you grow, you can become more sophisticated in your planning. You can prepare a more exhaustive business plan before you expand or make a significantly large investment in your business.

You can use a computer to write your business plan.

DESCRIPTION OF THE BUSINESS

The first part of a business plan is a description of your business. What will the business do? Who will be doing it? Where will it be done? For the ceramics business, you might write that you will be creating ceramic pieces with custom designs. You will be the one doing the work. It will be done at the local ceramics store.

The description should include your form of business ownership. This refers to whether your business is a corporation, an LLC, a partnership, or a sole proprietorship (also known as a Schedule C business). You can speak to a lawyer or tax accountant, or read about the different types of businesses on the Internal Revenue Service (IRS) Web site (http://www.irs.gov) or in books to learn more.

Most likely you'll begin as a sole proprietor. This means that you and the business are one entity: the money the business makes is the money you make. You must report your income on your federal tax return. You will also need to fill out and attach a Schedule C form for your business activity. (Depending on the amount of your earnings and expenses, you may be able to fill out a Schedule C-EZ, a simplified version of the form.)

If you plan to use a name other than your own for your business, in most states you are required to register that name. This fictitious name is known as your DBA ("doing business as") name. Registering a DBA name is done through your county clerk's office or through your state government. The Web site of the U.S. Small Business Administration (http://www.sba.gov) provides information about the process. Of course, you'll want to think of a name that is memorable and gives customers a clear idea of your service or product.

POTENTIAL CUSTOMERS AND COMPETITION

Who are your intended customers? What competition will you have? These are important parts of your business plan. If you can't identify your potential customers, how are you going to get them to buy your work? If you're unaware of your competition, how do you know you can successfully compete? Your potential customers might include people who are buying birthday or holiday gifts, people who are decorating their home, people who are getting married, or people who have a new baby.

Your competition consists of the other companies that offer a similar product or service. For the ceramics business, your competition may be online. Your competition may also include department stores, gift shops, and other stores that offer the type of dishware you have in mind. Check out what they are selling. One advantage you have is that you're a local artist with unique goods. Chances are, your work will be different enough that these larger stores will not be competing directly with you.

Check out the competition. Think of ways your work will differ.

MARKETING AND SALES

Your plan should include your strategies for informing people about your business and generating sales. For example, you might contact local decorators to see if they are interested in custom work for their clients. You might prepare a flyer to be displayed in the offices or gift shops of local houses of worship. Asking the hospital gift shop to display your flyer might be a good way to reach new parents.

How many pieces do you plan to create each month? How confident are you that you can sell these pieces? These are important questions to consider. It might be a good idea to start out with a few confirmed orders in hand. In any case, you'll need more than a hunch, guess, or good feeling about how many customers you'll have. You'll need to have a plan in place to meet with or attract customers and a good reason to believe your plan is going to work.

Many people do an Internet search for the services they need. Because of this, it's important to have a presence on the Internet. You can start with a free Facebook page and a blog for your business. Check out some keyword ranking sites and see which terms related to your product or service rank high in the search engines. Be sure to use those terms in your description of your business, as well as in your posts. Don't forget to include photos of your work. Invite friends and relatives to "like" your business page to help spread the word.

BUDGET

A budget is important for a new business enterprise. It should list all the items you will need to spend money on. For example, if you are making flyers you'll need to include paper; copying services or ink cartridges; tacks, staples, or adhesive putty; and any other necessary supplies. If you intend to print business cards, those costs should be included. If you plan to package

Keeping track of all money in and all money out is vital to a successful business.

items in special boxes or with a sticker that has your company's name on it, you need to include those costs, too. The fees for shipping or delivering products to customers are another key cost.

Some of your costs will be the same no matter how many customers you have. For instance, printing business cards is going to cost a certain amount no matter what. Other costs are going to depend on how many pieces you produce or customers you have. For instance, each ceramic piece will have a cost that includes studio time and materials. The more pieces you make, the higher the cost. Separate your budget into two parts. One will have the costs that don't vary. These are known as fixed costs. The other will have the costs that do vary. These are known as variable costs.

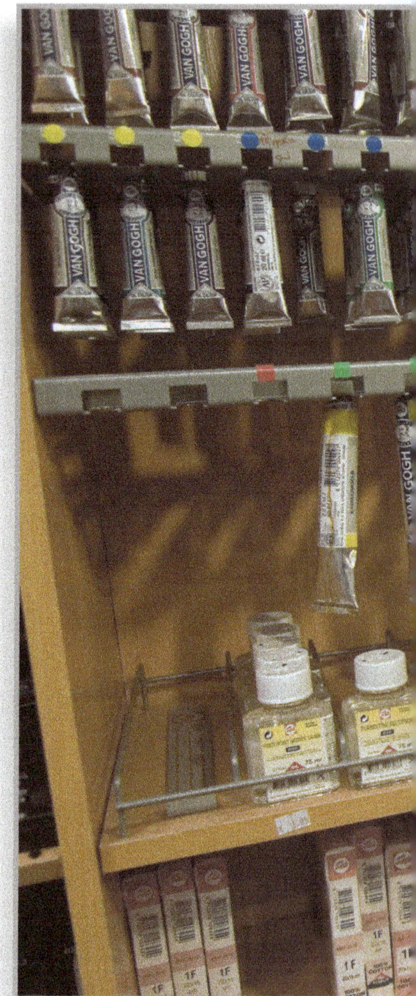

PRICE POINT AND PROFIT

Your price point is a vital piece of your business plan. If your work is priced too high, you may not generate enough sales volume to cover all of your costs. If your work is priced too low, you may have a large number of orders but lose money on each one. That's why it's important to determine the profit you will make on each piece.

The profit is the amount of money you make after all of your costs are covered. Let's say a large bowl costs you $25 to make. That amount includes the cost of materials and the fee for the time at the ceramics shop. If you sell the bowl for $25, you cover your costs for the bowl, but you make no money for

Don't forget to include the cost of supplies in the amount you charge customers for your products or services.

your labor. You also have no money to help pay for the flyers you made to advertise your business or any other start-up costs.

As the business owner, you need to decide how much more than $25 to charge. One way of doing that is to take all

KEEPING YOUR CUSTOMERS HAPPY

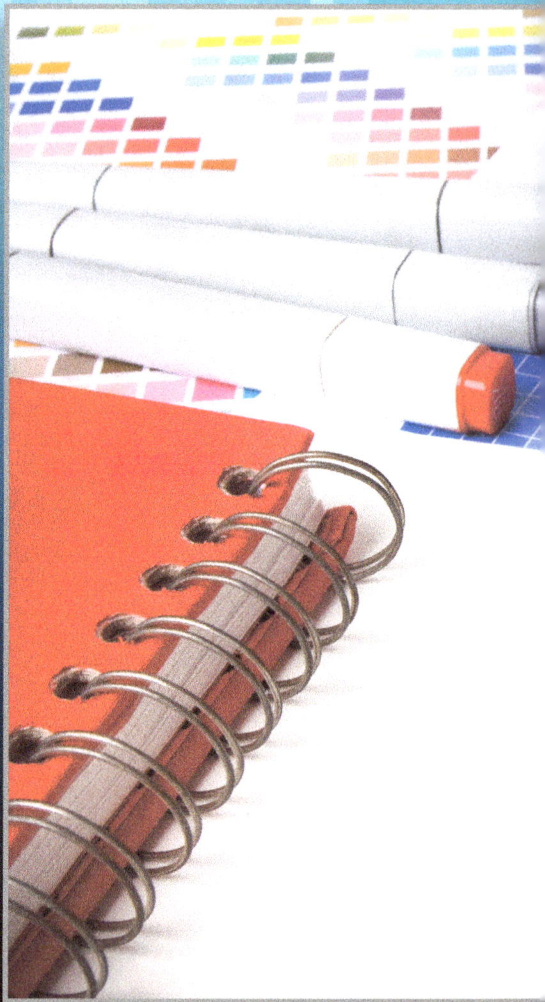

It's easier to keep a client than it is to find a new client. You want your clients to use you again. You also want them to tell their friends and relatives about you. Fortunately, keeping clients happy isn't difficult if you plan ahead and spell everything out in a signed agreement.

The most important step is to make sure everyone agrees on what the finished product will look like before you begin. As an artist, you'll need to sketch the design for the finished product. Get the client's signature on the sketch to show that he or she approved the design. Include samples of the colors and materials you have in mind. If you want to change something along the way, make sure your client approves the change.

Agree on the dates when each major part of the project will be completed. Include those dates in your written agreement. If you need the customer to do something—like clear a room of furniture—before you begin, make sure that is included in your agreement.

The most important part of good customer service is treating your customers the way you would like to be treated. If you are

Be certain to provide many details about the look of the finished product before the work begins.

working in a client's home, use drop cloths if necessary to protect floors and carpets. Clean up at the end of each day. Be sure you don't leave anything behind that could hurt a child or pet. Most of all, deliver the product you agreed to on time.

your general business costs (other than the costs of making the piece) and divide them by the number of pieces you plan to sell. By taking this overhead and including it in the price for each piece, you will be sure you cover all your costs. You also need to include an amount that is your profit.

When all is said and done, it's possible that a bowl that costs you $25 to make will sell for $40 or more. If you set the price at $40, you will make $15 on each bowl. Of course, not all of that is yours to keep. Part of that amount will go to cover your business costs. After all your costs are covered, the money that remains will be pure profit.

To decide how much to charge, it can be helpful to look at how much money you are investing to start your business. For instance, if you are investing $500, you will spend some of that amount on marketing and office supplies. Some will go toward making any samples you want to have on hand. That money will also pay for your portfolio. If you know you want to make back the $500 you've already spent, cover the cost of the items you'll create for your customers, and have a bit of money that is profit, you're well on the way to coming up with a selling price that will work.

Be aware that when doing custom work, you can ask your customers for a deposit at the start of a project. This can help you cover the cost of art supplies. For example, you can ask for 50 percent in the beginning and 50 percent at the end.

KEEPING TRACK OF INFORMATION

A big part of running a business is keeping track of information. You need to be diligent about tracking all of the money coming in and money going out. You also need to keep track of your clients and projects.

The simplest way to track your first customers is to create a record for each customer. It could be an index card with all the information about that customer and that project. It could be a record in a database application or a row in a spreadsheet. Use whatever makes the most sense to you.

Keep copies of your client agreements in a notebook, paper file, or computer folder where you can get to them easily. Use a calendar to track when any money is due to you. Make a note in green so you know it's about money coming in. If someone is more than a week late in paying you, politely call or e-mail to remind him or her.

Keep a copy of any invoices you need to pay. Store them using the same method you use for your client agreements. Mark your calendar in red to remind yourself of payments that must be mailed by a certain date to reach your vendors in time.

All of this information will help you in keeping your business running smoothly. It will also be important when it is time to pay income taxes. Ask an adult with experience to help you the first time you have taxes to pay. If you can't find anyone, at tax time there are often volunteers at the local library who can help you out.

CHAPTER 5

CONVERTING EXPERIENCE INTO SUCCESS

By now you've probably realized that getting experience isn't the ultimate goal. Using your experience to jump-start your success—either as a small business owner or as an employee in a job that uses artistic skills—is the ultimate goal. Somehow you must bridge the gap between your first work experiences and your dream career.

The key to this transition lies with you. You are the one who is most interested in your success. You know best what you like and don't like to do. You are also in the best position to identify the kinds of workplaces where you feel most comfortable and the job responsibilities that would make you look forward to working.

The following sections discuss how you can use your experience to help you land a job, gain admission to a college or art program, or start a thriving business.

FIRST STEPS

You may think you'll remember the details of all of your volunteer positions or part-time jobs. But it is easy to forget. The best thing to do is to create an index card, computer file, or notebook page with the details of each job. Do this as soon as your job is finished, if not before. Include your responsibilities, how long the project took, and the key people you worked with. Record the contact information for the supervisor to whom you reported. If you have a letter of recommendation from a project or job, keep it in the file or notebook with the rest of the information about it. Be sure

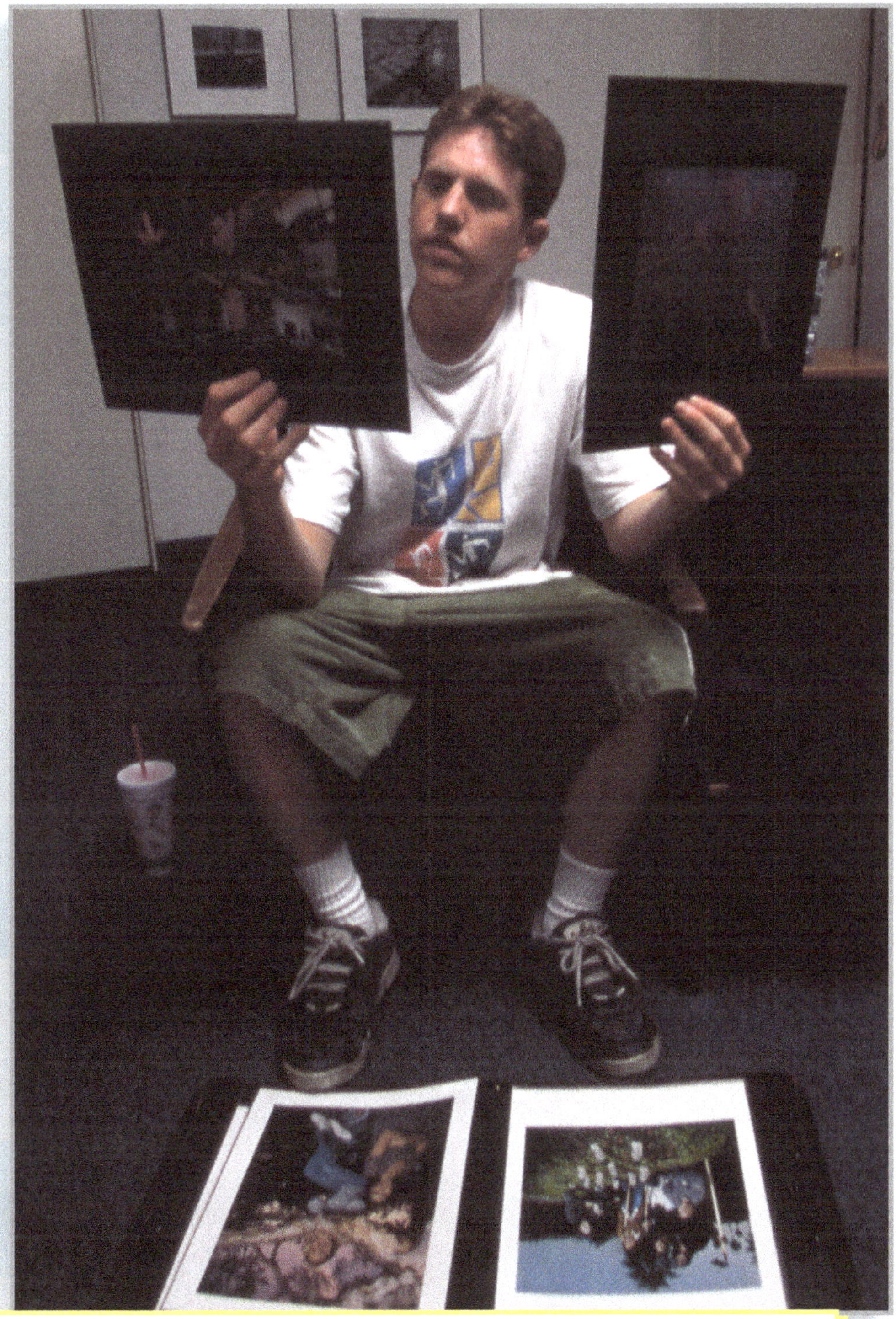

Pick items for your portfolio that communicate your unique vision as an artist.

to take photos of the finished work, too, and keep it with the other materials.

While you are working at a position, remember to ask if you can use your supervisor as a reference. Also take any opportunity to talk about possible career options with each employer. Your supervisors may know about types of jobs that are new to you. These jobs may use your artistic talents in ways that fit you perfectly. They also may know of interesting summer or university programs that will help you launch your career. You won't know unless you politely ask for a bit of their time and tell them about what you hope to accomplish in the art field.

In the arts, your portfolio is vital to your success. You may include different items, depending on the opportunity, but be sure to include samples of your work that showcase your abilities and creativity. The items you include should give a good idea of who you are as an artist. Your portfolio should also include a summary of your experience, letters of recommendation, and references.

APPLYING TO ACADEMIC PROGRAMS

Just the thought of writing an essay for admission to an academic program is enough to make most of us sweat. It needs to be well written. It needs to be impressive. It needs to be succinct. It needs to be brilliant. (No pressure!)

In truth, the admission essay is an excellent opportunity to turn your experience into success. In many cases, applicants are asked to write several essays. Make sure one of your essays is about the things you've learned as you've gained experience in the field. Describe the steps you've taken to find jobs and

Find a way to include your experiences as an artistic teen in your applications for college or other endeavors.

experiences that draw upon your artistic talents. Talk about the challenging and rewarding parts of those experiences. Discuss what you've gained as a result of your determination and creativity. Above all, be sure your essay highlights your experience while giving the admissions officers a sense of who you are.

NETWORKING

Chances are, you've heard a lot of talk about networking. Networking involves talking to people—doing informational interviews, meeting people for tea or coffee, or taking people to lunch. Networking is an excellent way to turn experience into success, especially for young people who are just starting out.

Networking can involve online professional networks, but it isn't just about social media. It is about speaking with people who can help you, or who can introduce you to others who can help you. Perhaps there is a successful small business in your town. The business may or may not have anything to do with art, but it offers a service and has many happy customers. Ask the owner if you can take her to lunch. Then ask her questions about her biggest challenges, the best ways she's found to attract customers, and the one thing she wishes she'd known before she started her business. You can learn a great deal from others who have blazed trails ahead of you, and this can decrease the time it takes you to reach your desired destination. Someday, you can return the favor by sharing your wisdom with another young hopeful.

Networking is a way for friends, or friends of friends, to help one another achieve a goal.

JOB SEEKING

Whether or not college is in your plans, you'll likely want to turn your experience into a paying job. The most important tools for landing a job are your portfolio and résumé, which should include a summary of your skills and experience. Be sure to include all of the significant work you've done, including experience you gained on your own. Include the length of time you worked at each position and your key achievements.

The interviewer will use your résumé to ask about your experience. Find a way to emphasize the experience that is most relevant to the artistic position you are seeking. Be polite, but don't be shy. An interview is one of your biggest chances to communicate positive information about yourself.

Don't be surprised if the interviewer asks you about your biggest mistakes or regrets. It's OK to admit that you have made errors. Keep the discussion light, and explain the way you fixed the situation or what you learned from it. The main point is to show that you've grown as a result of a negative experience.

If the questions you're asked don't provide the opportunity for you to stress your artistic talents and experience, stay calm. At the end of the interview, say that you'd like to mention your reasons for applying for the job. Take that opportunity to speak briefly about your talents, your experience, and the role you hope to play at the company.

LEARNING ABOUT BUSINESS

You're young. You're serious about starting and running your own business. You've read every book and article you can find. What other ways are there for you to learn more before you start your business?

Ideally, you'll find opportunities to learn about running a business before you launch your own. Joining a teen entrepreneurs' club is one way to start.

Does your school have a club for aspiring entrepreneurs? Does it have a Junior Achievement program? If so, these could be good ways for you to get information and support as you plan and launch your business. If there isn't a club for entrepreneurial teens, now might be the perfect time to start one. Be sure to invite professionals from organizations involved in the arts to speak at the club.

Youth groups such as 4-H and scouting offer programs of interest to those starting businesses. For instance, 4-H offers a curriculum in entrepreneurship. The Boy Scouts of America offers merit badges in entrepreneurship and salesmanship. Girl Scouts of the USA has a number of business-oriented badges, too. Local chambers of commerce and local arts guilds may offer support to entrepreneurial teens as well.

The U.S. Small Business Administration (SBA) offers helpful information for teens. A number of magazines focus on entrepreneurs and small businesses. Although most of their readers are adults, the advice and information they print applies to any small business owner. That includes you!

GLOSSARY

BRAINSTORMING A process for creative thinking in which an individual or group comes up with as many possible solutions to a problem as possible in a given amount of time.

BUDGET A plan for expenditures and income for a period of time.

BUSINESS An enterprise that is started with the intention of making a profit.

BUSINESS PLAN A plan for business success that includes costs, competition, estimates of sales activity, marketing strategies, and other important details.

CONSIGNMENT The act of placing goods with a dealer who will sell those goods on the condition that he or she will keep a percentage of the sales price as a commission.

CURATOR A person who manages or oversees the collections of a museum, art gallery, or similar institution.

ENTREPRENEUR A person who starts and runs a business of his or her own.

HOBBY An activity a person engages in for enjoyment or relaxation.

INITIAL INVESTMENT The amount of money that is needed to start a business.

INTERNSHIP A temporary job placement that allows a person to get hands-on experience in a career field. An internship can be paid or unpaid.

INVOICE A statement listing the goods delivered or services provided and the amount due for them; bill.

LICENSING A contractual agreement that gives one or more companies permission to produce and sell products incorporating the design, artwork, or logo of another company.

LIMITED LIABILITY COMPANY (LLC) A business structure available in most states that protects its owners from personal responsibility for company debts that exceed the amount the owners have invested.

MARKETING The action of promoting and selling products or services.

MOSAIC A decorative work made by setting small pieces of colored glass, tile, or stone into another material to create a picture or pattern.

MURAL A piece of artwork that is painted or directly applied to a large surface such as a wall or ceiling.

NICHE A specialized but profitable section of the market.

PITCH A line of talk designed to persuade.

REFERENCE A person who is in a position to speak about a candidate's qualifications for a job and has agreed to do so.

REVENUE The income earned from a company's sales of products or services to its customers.

SALES VOLUME The quantity of total sales in a given period.

SCHEDULE C The federal tax form used to report business income or business losses for a sole proprietor, independent contractor, or self-employed individual.

SOLE PROPRIETORSHIP An unincorporated business with one owner who pays personal income tax on profits from the business.

TRANSFERABLE SKILLS Abilities and personal qualities a worker can use in more than one occupation.

VENDOR A person or company that provides goods and services to a business; supplier.

FOR MORE INFORMATION

Canadian Youth Business Foundation (CYBF)
100 Adelaide Street West
Suite 1302
Toronto, ON M5H 1S3
Canada
(866) 646-2922
Web site: http://www.cybf.ca
The Canadian Youth Business Foundation provides guidance, investment, community, and a voice to young entrepreneurs in Canada.

The Center for Entrepreneurship
John Cook School of Business
Saint Louis University
3674 Lindell Boulevard, Suite DS-100
Saint Louis, MO 63108
(314) 977-3850
Web site: http://www.slu.edu/924-teen-entrepreneur-symposium
The Center for Entrepreneurship at the John Cook School of Business is a national leader in developing and delivering innovative programs to promote entrepreneurship through education. Its mission is to deliver and develop world-class education in entrepreneurship for all.

CITYarts, Inc.
525 Broadway, Suite 602
New York, NY 10012
(212) 966-0377
Web site: http://www.cityarts.org
CITYarts brings young people and professional artists together to create public art. Through this creative process, CITYarts

empowers youth and children to become active participants in transforming communities. The organization also identifies artistically talented youth and offers a range of support, including career advice and recommendations on higher education choices.

Dingman Center for Entrepreneurship

Robert H. Smith School of Business at the University of Maryland
2518 Van Munching Hall
College Park, MD 20742
(301) 405-9545
Web site: http://www.rhsmith.umd.edu/dingman

This center offers a variety of programs for people interested in launching businesses. It provides experiential learning opportunities to help young entrepreneurs build their ventures.

Independent Youth

10632 S. Memorial Drive
P.O. Box 330196
Tulsa, OK 74133
(877) 617-0494
Web site: http://www.independentyouth.org

Independent Youth is a nonprofit organization that helps young people ages twelve to eighteen become successful entrepreneurs. The organization generates entrepreneurial awareness and understanding through an array of educational programs and hands-on experiences, including Webinars, student trainings, and internships.

Institute of Contemporary Art/Boston (ICA)

100 Northern Avenue
Boston, MA 02210
(617) 478-3100
Web site: http://www.icaboston.org

The ICA offers a variety of programs for high school students interested in art, led by its Teen Arts Council (TAC). This group of motivated teens plans creative events and opportunities at the museum, including artist talks, workshops, performances, art-making activities, and more.

Junior Achievement USA
One Education Way
Colorado Springs, CO 80906
(719) 540-8000
Web site: http://www.ja.org
Junior Achievement educates youth about entrepreneurship and financial literacy through experiential, hands-on programs. Its programs show young people how to generate wealth and effectively manage it, how to create jobs that make their communities more robust, and how to apply entrepreneurial thinking to the workplace.

Network for Teaching Entrepreneurship
120 Wall Street, 18th Floor
New York, NY 10005
(212) 232-3333
Web site: http://www.nfte.com
The Network for Teaching Entrepreneurship provides programs that inspire young people to stay in school, to recognize business opportunities, and to plan for successful futures.

Shunpike
3518 Fremont Avenue North, Box 118
Seattle, WA 98103
(206) 905-1026
Web site: http://www.shunpike.org
Shunpike provides training, support, and networking opportunities for today's and tomorrow's arts entrepreneurs.

U.S. Small Business Administration—Teen Business Link
409 3rd Street SW
Washington, DC 20416
(800) 827-5722
Web site: http://archive.sba.gov/teens
The Small Business Administration's Teen Business Link site has information that applies directly to teens who are interested in starting a business. It includes a section on avoiding legal problems.

WEB SITES

Due to the changing nature of Internet links, Rosen Publishing has developed an online list of Web sites related to the subject of this book. This site is updated regularly. Please use this link to access this list:

http://www.rosenlinks.com/MMN/Art

FOR FURTHER READING

Bradshaw, Maddie. *Maddie Bradshaw's You Can Start a Business, Too!* Austin, TX: m3 Girl Designs, 2010.

Carey, Brainard. *New Markets for Artists: How to Sell, Fund Projects, and Exhibit Using Social Media, DIY Pop-Ups, eBay, Kickstarter, and Much More.* New York, NY: Allworth Press, 2012.

Donovan, Sandra. *Job Smarts: How to Find Work or Start a Business, Manage Earnings, and More* (*USA TODAY* Teen Wise Guides). Minneapolis, MN: Twenty-First Century Books, 2012.

Ferguson Publishing. *Discovering Careers: Art.* New York, NY: Ferguson, 2012.

Fischer, Kristen. *When Talent Isn't Enough: Business Basics for the Creatively Inclined.* Pompton Plains, NJ: Career Press, 2013.

McDougall, J. S. *Start Your Own Arts and Crafts Business: Retail, Carts and Kiosks, Craft Shows, Street Fairs.* Irvine, CA: Entrepreneur Press, 2007.

Pinkney, Andrea Davis, and Amy Rosen. *Teen Business Blasts Off!* New York, NY: Network for Teaching Entrepreneurship; Scholastic, Inc., 2010.

Rankin, Kenrya. *Start It Up: The Complete Teen Business Guide for Turning Your Passions into Pay.* San Francisco, CA: Zest Books, 2011.

Reeves, Diane Lindsey, Lindsey Clasen, and Nancy Bond. *Career Ideas for Kids Who Like Art.* 2nd ed. New York, NY: Ferguson, 2007.

Rogers, Lilla. *I Just Like to Make Things: Learn the Secrets to Making Money While Staying Passionate About Your Art and Craft*. Beverly, MA: Quarry Books, 2013.

Schwake, Susan, and Rainer Schwake. *Art Lab for Kids: 52 Creative Adventures in Drawing, Painting, Printmaking, Paper, and Mixed Media—For Budding Artists of All Ages*. Beverly, MA: Quarry Books, 2012.

Searle, Teresa. *Fabric Jewelry: 25 Designs to Make Using Silk, Ribbon, Buttons, and Beads*. New York, NY: St. Martin's Griffin, 2008.

Simons, Rae. *Entrepreneurship* (Junior Library of Money). Broomall, PA: Mason Crest Publishers, 2011.

Spinks-Burleson, Kimberly, and Robyn Collins. *Prepare to Be a Teen Millionaire*. Deerfield Beach, FL: Health Communications, Inc., 2008.

Toren, Adam, Matthew Toren, and Turonny Foo. *Kidpreneur$: Young Entrepreneurs with Big Ideas!* Phoenix, AZ: Business Plus Media Group, 2009.

BIBLIOGRAPHY

Abrams, Rhonda M. *The Successful Business Plan: Secrets & Strategies.* Palo Alto, CA: Planning Shop, 2003.

Bolles, Richard Nelson. *What Color Is Your Parachute? A Practical Manual for Job-Hunters and Career-Changers.* Berkeley, CA: Ten Speed Press, 2011.

Boy Scouts of America. "Introduction to Merit Badges." 2012. Retrieved September 1, 2012 (http://www.scouting.org/meritbadges.aspx).

Bygrave, William D., and Andrew Zacharakis. *Entrepreneurship.* 2nd ed. Hoboken, NJ: Wiley, 2011.

Christen, Carol, Richard Nelson Bolles, and Jean M. Blomquist. *What Color Is Your Parachute? For Teens: Discovering Yourself, Defining Your Future.* 2nd ed. Berkeley, CA: Ten Speed Press, 2010.

DeBaise, Colleen. *The Wall Street Journal Complete Small Business Guidebook.* New York, NY: Three Rivers Press, 2009.

Everett, Robert F. *The Entrepreneur's Guide to Marketing.* Westport, CT: Praeger, 2009.

Ewing Marion Kauffman Foundation. "Youth Entrepreneurship Survey 2010." 2012. Retrieved September 1, 2012 (http://www.kauffman.org/entrepreneurship/youth-entrepreneurship-survey-2010.aspx).

Greene, Cynthia L. *Entrepreneurship* (21st Century Business). Mason, OH: South-Western Cengage Learning, 2011.

Hiser, Kevin. "Why Your Business Plan Is Probably Incomplete." YoungEntrepreneur.com, August 9, 2012.

Retrieved August 28, 2012 (http://www.youngentrepreneur.com/blog/why-your-business-plan-is-probably-incomplete).

Holzner, Steven. *Small Business Web Sites Made Easy.* New York, NY: McGraw-Hill, 2009.

Levinson, Jay Conrad, Jeannie Levinson, and Amy Levinson. *Guerrilla Marketing: Easy and Inexpensive Strategies for Making Big Profits from Your Small Business.* 4th ed. Boston, MA: Houghton Mifflin, 2007.

McKeever, Mike P. *How to Write a Business Plan.* 9th ed. Berkeley, CA: Nolo, 2008.

National 4-H Cooperative Curriculum System, Inc. "Entrepreneurship." Retrieved September 2, 2012 (http://new.4-hcurriculum.org/projects/entrepreneur).

National Service-Learning Clearinghouse. "Frequently Asked Questions (FAQs)." 2012. Retrieved August 30, 2012 (http://www.servicelearning.org/faq).

Porter, Jane. "How to Build Credibility as a Young Entrepreneur." Entrepreneur.com, August 8, 2011. Retrieved October 9, 2012 (http://www.entrepreneur.com/article/220119).

Porter, Michael E. *Competitive Advantage: Creating and Sustaining Superior Performance.* New York, NY: Free Press, 1985.

Scarborough, Norman M., Doug Wilson, and Thomas Zimmerer. *Essentials of Entrepreneurship and Small Business Management.* 6th ed. Upper Saddle River, NJ: Prentice Hall, 2011.

Stephenson, James, and Courtney Thurman. *Ultimate Small Business Marketing Guide: 1500 Great Marketing Tricks That Will Drive Your Business Through the Roof.* 2nd ed. Irvine, CA: Entrepreneur Press, 2007.

U.S. Department of Labor. "I Am 18." Youth Rules. Retrieved September 2, 2012 (http://www.youthrules.dol.gov/know-the-limits/18.htm).

U.S. Department of Labor. "I Am 14 or 15." Youth Rules. Retrieved September 1, 2012 (http://www.youthrules.dol.gov/know-the-limits/14-15.htm).

U.S. Department of Labor. "I Am 16 or 17." Youth Rules. Retrieved August 31, 2012 (http://www.youthrules.dol.gov/know-the-limits/16-17.htm).

U.S. Department of Labor, Wage and Hour Division. "Child Labor Provisions for Nonagricultural Occupations Under the Fair Labor Standards Act." July 2010. Retrieved July 10, 2012 (http://www.dol.gov/whd/regs/compliance/childlabor101_text.htm).

U.S. Small Business Administration. "Put It In Writing." Teen Business Link. Retrieved August 30, 2012 (http://archive.sba.gov/teens/myplan.html).

YouTube.com. "The Nate Berkus Show—February 10, 2011." 2011. Retrieved July 10, 2012 (http://www.youtube.com/watch?v=G3Cn6jApCnM).

INDEX

ABOUT THE AUTHOR

Gina Hagler is an award-winning author. She has an MBA and has started several successful small businesses. She has also worked as a small business consultant. She writes on a variety of topics for children and adults. One of her favorite topics is entrepreneurship.

PHOTO CREDITS

Cover, p. 8 Chuck Rausin/Shutterstock.com; p. 5 Linda Raymond Photography/Flickr/Getty Images; pp. 10–11 Ariel Skelley/Photographer's Choice/Getty Images; p. 13 © AP Images; pp. 14–15 Picsfive/Shutterstock.com; pp. 16–17 Mandy Godbehear/Shutterstock.com; pp. 20–21 Stockbyte/Thinkstock; pp. 24–25 Paul Strowger/Flickr/Getty Images; p. 28 Peter Dazeley/Photographer's Choice/Getty Images; p. 30 iStockphoto/Thinkstock; p. 33 Blend Images/John Lund/Marc Romanelli/the Agency Collection/Getty Images; p. 35 Leah-Anne Thompson/Shutterstock.com; pp. 38–39 MANIN Richard/hemis.fr/Getty Images; p. 41 Hill Street Studios/Eric Raptosh/Blend Images/Getty Images; pp. 44–45 Robert Daly/OJO Images/Getty Images; pp. 46–47 Andrew Gentry/Shutterstock.com; p. 49 Reggie Casagrande/The Image Bank/Getty Images; pp. 50–51 age fotostock/SuperStock; pp. 52–53 joingate/Shutterstock.com; p. 57 © Davis Barber/PhotoEdit; pp. 58–59 Don Bayley/E+/Getty Images; pp. 60–61 mediaphotos/E+/Getty Images; p. 63 Alexander Raths/Shutterstock.com; pp. 3, 4, 65–80 (background image), page borders, boxed text backgrounds © iStockphoto.com/Tomasz Sowinski; back cover and remaining interior background image © iStockphoto.com/Pavel Khorenyan.

Designer: Brian Garvey; Editor: Andrea Sclarow Paskoff; Photo Researcher: Karen Huang